Sojourner Truth

W. Terry Whalin

Illustrated by
Ken Landgraf

BARBOUR
PUBLISHING, INC.
Uhrichsville, Ohio

© MCMXCIX by Barbour Publishing, Inc.

ISBN 1-57748-515-7

All rights reserved. No part of this publication may be repro-
duced or transmitted in any form or by any means without
written permission of the publisher.

Published by Barbour Publishing, Inc., P.O. Box 719,
Uhrichsville, Ohio 44683 http://www.barbourbooks.com

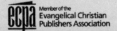

Member of the
Evangelical Christian
Publishers Association

Printed in the United States of America.

Sojourner
Truth

COLONEL HARDENBERGH MADE HIS
CUSTOMARY VISIT TO SLAVE QUARTERS.

1

Around 1797 on a farm near the Hudson River in upstate New York, Colonel Johannes Hardenbergh made his customary visit to the slave quarters. Any time there was a new birth on his plantation—a calf, a lamb, or a slave— the colonel wanted to inspect that which had increased the value of his property. This time, it was the birth of a child named Isabella. (Since records were not kept of slave births, some people claim Isabella was born in either 1776 or 1777, but 1797 is more reasonable.) Colonel Hardenbergh approved of the choice of her name, but her parents, James and Betsey, called the girl Belle.

"She has strong arms," the owner told the parents in Low Dutch. "She'll make a good worker." Colonel Hardenbergh spoke English when he conducted his business, but at home he preferred to speak the language of his ancestors, Dutch. Dutch descendants like Colonel Hardenbergh learned English, but they clung to their native language. The slaves on the colonel's farm didn't have the opportunity to learn English, so they spoke and understood only Dutch. Language was another way to control the slaves since they couldn't communicate with the majority of the people around them.

Belle's father was a tall, strong man who was proud of his ability to do hard work. James was called Baumfree, a Low Dutch word which means "tree." The years of hard work had taken

6

BELLE'S FATHER WAS A STRONG MAN.

a toll on this big man. Betsey, Belle's mother, was a big, stocky woman with large hands. She was called Mau Mau Brett. Mau Mau Brett was much younger than Baumfree, but they loved each other and had a good marriage. Each of their ten previous children had died or been sold into slavery. As a matter of fact, slaves had been bought and sold on farms throughout this area of New York for the last 150 years. Now Belle's parents worried that she might be sold as well.

Slavery cast a long shadow over the lives of slave parents and their children. Often children were taken from their families and sold. Slave parents did not have many opportunities to prepare their children for the difficulties of being a slave. Knowing this, at an early age, Belle's parents taught her obedience because a disobedient slave was often punished harshly. Her parents also instilled in Belle the importance of hard work, honesty, and loyalty. Another value

BELLE'S MOTHER WAS CALLED
MAU MAU BRETT.

they taught was suffering in silence. "Never make a fuss in front of the white folk," her mother told Belle. "When you've got to cry, cry alone."

When Belle was about three years old, Colonel Hardenbergh died. His son, Charles, had recently built a large limestone house in the nearby hills. He claimed and moved his inheritance of livestock and ten slaves, including Isabella and her parents. Charles, however, provided no slave housing on this new property; instead he moved his slaves into the damp cellar of his stone house. The ten slaves had no privacy in this room where they ate and slept.

Soon after Isabella and her parents moved to the Charles Hardenbergh farm, her brother Peter was born. Now there was someone else to love—Peter. One night when both children were still very young, their mother took them outside and sat them under a tree. "My children," she said to them, "there is a God who

THE TEN SLAVES ATE AND SLEPT
IN THE CELLAR.

hears and sees you." The two small children looked around them but they couldn't see God.

"Where does God live?" Belle asked her mother.

"He lives in the sky," their mother answered, "and when you are beaten, or cruelly treated, or fall into any trouble, you must ask His help. He will always hear and help you." Their mother promised the children that they were under God's protection.

Sometimes Belle had to face some difficult lessons in her young life. One night, she heard her mother crying. "What's wrong, Mau Mau?" Belle gently asked.

"I'm groaning to think of my poor children," Mau Mau said. "They don't know where I be, and I don't know where they be. They look up at the stars, and I look up at the stars, but I can't tell where they be."

Later her mother told Belle how, many years earlier, Michael and Nancy, an older

"WHERE DOES GOD LIVE?"

brother and sister, had been snatched from their family. One snowy winter morning, some men in a horse-drawn sled stopped at the cabin where Isabella's family lived. Michael was delighted when the men told him that he was going for a ride on the sled. Quickly the boy jumped onto the sled, but a few minutes later, his joy turned into fear. One of the men walked out of the cabin with a large box which contained his sister, Nancy. She was screaming.

Afraid of these men, Michael jumped off the sled, ran inside the cabin, and hid under a bed. The men came into the cabin, dragged Michael outside, put him on the sled, then drove away. Isabella's parents were helpless to stop these slave traders. Their master had sold these children. They never saw Michael or Nancy again.

Despite her mother's fears that Belle would be snatched away and sold to someone else, the family remained together until Isabella was

THE MAN DROVE AWAY ON A SLED.

about eleven years old. In 1808, Charles Hardenbergh suddenly died, and his heirs decided to auction off his horses, cattle, and slaves.

The day of the auction, the Stone Ridge Farm was crowded with people. Belle stood trembling beside her mother. "I don't want to leave you, Mau Mau! What if they beat me? Why can't I go free like you and Baumfree?"

"Hush, Belle," her mother said softly in Dutch.

Then Belle's father, Baumfree, said, "Nobody would buy a broken-down old horse like me. The law says Old Master's kin have to take care of me, so they're letting me and Mau Mau go free to get rid of us."

Almost thirty years earlier, a New York law had been passed that allowed any slave over fifty years old to be freed, but this law also required that the freed slave be able to earn a living. From living in the damp cellar, Baumfree

THE STONE RIDGE FARM WAS
CROWDED WITH PEOPLE.

had developed arthritis which disfigured his legs and hands. Now he was unable to work. Even so, Hardenbergh's heirs decided to free both Baumfree and Mau Mau. Younger and in better health, Mau Mau could support both of them. The couple was allowed to continue living in the dark cellar as long as Mau Mau continued to work for the family. Baumfree and Mau Mau had no choice but to accept the offer. These old slaves didn't speak any English and couldn't function in the world beyond the farm.

With tears in her eyes, Mau Mau told Belle some last words. "Child, you can't stay with us. All our other children were sold. Now it's your turn and your little brother's."

"Just remember what we've taught you, Belle," Baumfree said. "Obey your master and work hard."

Mau Mau chimed in, saying, "And if you pray to God, He'll see that you're treated right."

A white man motioned for Belle. It was

A WHITE MAN MOTIONED FOR BELLE.

time for her to be auctioned. "Good-bye, Mau Mau. Good-bye, Baumfree."

Belle and her brother Peter stood in the auction area. Peter was sold first to a man who didn't live in the area. Although Belle felt like crying, she stood in stony silence. Over and over in her head, Belle repeated the Lord's Prayer.

The auctioneer called out, "Hardenbergh's Belle, age eleven, good strong body." The girl couldn't understand the words since they were in English, but she knew it meant that she was being sold. At first no one in the crowd offered to bid.

Belle dared to hope. *Maybe I will be allowed to stay on the farm with my parents*, she thought.

Then the auctioneer ordered Belle to turn to the right. When the girl didn't move, the man grabbed her and physically turned her. "Look how tall she is, even now. She'll be a big woman in maturity, have lots of children, and be able to do a lot of work."

THE AUCTIONEER ORDERED BELLE
TO TURN TO THE RIGHT.

Still no one offered to buy Belle. Then the auctioneer threw in a flock of sheep saying, "They go with the girl." John Neely, a shopkeeper from Kingston Landing, New York, stood in the audience and recognized a bargain that he couldn't pass up. He offered $100 and, with a crack from the auctioneer's gavel, the sheep and Belle were sold.

While Neely thought he had struck a good deal, his wife didn't. "This girl can't speak English," she yelled at her husband. "Sure she looks strong, but what good is she for me? When I ask for a pot, she gives me a spoon. When I ask for a skillet, she hands me a broom."

One day Mrs. Neely's frustrations grew until she couldn't stand it anymore. This Sunday morning, she sent her slave out to the barn. In the barn, Belle found Mr. Neely heating some metal rods over red-hot coals. Without offering any explanation, Mr. Neely grabbed Belle's hands and tied them together. He tore Belle's shirt off,

BELLE AND THE SHEEP WERE SOLD.

then began to beat the girl's back. Belle pleaded with her master to stop, calling out to God for help until she finally fainted. It was her first beating, and she determined never to experience another one.

After about two years with the Neelys, Martin Schryver purchased Belle from the Neelys for $105. This fisherman didn't own any other slaves but had a farm and a tavern on the Roundout River. This new location was only about five miles from the Neelys' farm. Belle soon learned that though the Schryvers were a coarse and uneducated couple, they weren't cruel. Since they spoke both English and Dutch, Belle could easily talk with them. Without someone yelling at her constantly, Belle quickly learned English, although it was marked with a strong Dutch accent.

In the meantime, her parents were doing poorly as freed slaves. They found it difficult to get enough food to eat and grew ill and old. Too

A FISHERMAN PURCHASED BELLE.

soon, Mau Mau Brett grew sick and died. Mr. Simmons, who was now renting Charles Hardenbergh's stone house, came to the Schryvers to take Belle to the funeral. He explained to Belle, "This past winter was very hard. One day Baumfree had gone out to do a small chore for pennies. When he returned to the cellar, he found Mau Mau in a coma. By morning, she'd died." Poor Baumfree was grief-stricken from his loss.

Despite her concern for her father, Belle couldn't do anything for Baumfree. She had to return to the Schryver family. She prayed that God would give her a means to help her father.

While working in the tavern, Belle overheard many conversations about slavery. Her ears perked up whenever the people began talking about abolition. It was a new English word that Belle had learned. The abolitionists were people who wanted to end slavery. While Belle didn't understand much about it, she knew that if she were free, she'd go straight to Baumfree.

BAUMFREE WAS GRIEF-STRICKEN.

"Whoever these abolitionists are, God," Belle prayed, "please bless their work."

Soon afterwards, Belle received a message that her father, Baumfree, had starved to death. Now, other than Peter, Belle had no known living immediate family. She felt alone; even God seemed so distant. In her own determined way, Belle decided to pray for the only thing left: her freedom. She remembered the words of Mau Mau about the great God in the sky, "God is always with you. You are never alone." Then she thought, *Perhaps the rumors that I hear are true. Maybe soon the slaves in New York will be freed.*

"GOD IS ALWAYS WITH YOU."

"I'LL BUY HER FOR $300."

2

One day, a short, ruddy-faced man came into the tavern. As Belle served the various customers, this man began a conversation with Mr. Schryver.

"That slave girl yours?" the man inquired.

"Yes. Belle is thirteen, and she'll grow to be well over six feet," Mr. Schryver said.

"I need this girl to help out on my farm in New Paltz," the man said. "I'll buy her for $300." The price was three times what the Schryvers had paid only a year and a half ago. Although the couple didn't approve of slavery and had plans to free Belle when she reached eighteen, $300 was a lot of money. The Schryvers accepted the offer, and Belle answered to a new master named John Dumont.

The farmer was pleased with his purchase and recorded in a book dated 1810, that Belle was "about thirteen," but "stands nearly six feet tall." When Belle came to the Dumonts' farm, the ten other slaves welcomed her. On most accounts, according to the slaves, Mr. Dumont was a decent man and didn't deal out excessive punishment. They said, "He doesn't believe in separating families, and if you do your work and don't make trouble, then you'll get along fine."

When the slaves began to talk about the mistress of the house, however, it was a completely different story. "Watch your step around Mrs. Dumont," they warned. "She's got a spiteful tongue and a sour temperament. As much as

THE SLAVES BEGAN TO TALK.

possible, keep away from her because it will only get you into trouble." But it was impossible for Belle to keep away from Mrs. Dumont because Belle worked part-time in the big house.

In fact, Mrs. Dumont took an instant dislike to her quiet-spoken new slave. Mrs. Dumont pulled her two white maids aside and told them, "Isabella should be taught a lesson. Make sure you grind down her proud attitude."

Despite the harsh treatment from her mistress and coworkers in the Dumont house, Belle remembered her mother's lessons on obedience and always tried hard to please her owners. Sometimes the other slaves chided Belle saying, "Girl, you're too obedient for Master and Miss Dumont."

Throughout her childhood, Belle had been taught to repay evil with good. She had developed a deep spiritual belief that her hard work would eventually be rewarded. During this period, Belle decided that her master Dumont

ISABELLA SHOULD BE TAUGHT A LESSON.

was a god. In her mind, she reasoned that if a god knows everything he must know about slavery. Convinced that her master was an all-seeing and all-knowing god, Belle was driven by fear.

Dumont often bragged about the hardworking Belle. "Why, she can do a good family's washing at night and be ready in the morning to go to the field and still do as much raking and binding as my best hands," he told his neighbors.

When the master talked about Belle in this manner, the other slaves grew impatient and critical of her. They called her the white peoples' pet, and drove her out of their circle of friends. The other slaves couldn't understand Belle's confusion and hurt.

One day, Cato, the Dumonts' driver, took Belle aside and said, "What's the matter with you, gal? Can't you see you only hurtin' the rest of us when you work yo'self to death like you doin'? Next thing we know, the master'll

CATO TOOK BELLE ASIDE.

be expectin' us all to work like that. Where'll we find the time to take care of our own children then? When is old people gonna rest? Workin' hard ain't gonna free any of us. Just kill us sooner, that's all."

From Cato, Belle began to understand that Dumont wasn't a god. And if he wasn't a god, then Belle didn't need to be afraid all of the time. She could talk to the great God in the sky without her master hearing her pleas for help and understanding.

With her changed attitude about Dumont, the other slaves on the farm began to trust Belle again, but she still felt lonely without any family around. Throughout her years with Dumont, Belle came to accept that loneliness would be her companion.

One day as John Dumont stood in the distance watching his slaves, he thought to himself, *It's time for Belle to get married and begin to have*

LONELINESS WOULD BE HER COMPANION.

children. Tom would make a good husband for her. Dumont had purchased Tom as a young man, and he had worked many years on the farm. To Dumont, it made no difference that Belle and Tom didn't love each other. They were just two slaves.

Belle could see that her husband had been a good-looking man at one time, but now he was stooped and old from his years of hard labor in the fields. In their own way, Tom and Belle came to love each other. Belle was considerate and caring for her husband, and Tom was quiet and agreeable. After a year of marriage, the couple had a daughter named Diana. During the next twelve years, Isabella gave birth to four more children: Elizabeth, Hannah, Peter, and Sophia. Each child learned the lessons that Belle had learned from her mother, Mau Mau Brett: never steal, never lie, and always obey your master.

Year after year, Belle chopped wood, planted

BELLE CHOPPED WOOD.

corn, and hauled buckets of water for the Dumonts. In the midst of hours of hard work, Belle never gave up hope that one day she would be free. In 1824, she finally learned the good news. Pressured by abolitionist groups, the New York state legislature had passed an emancipation law. The law required that all slaves born before July 4, 1799, be freed on July 4, 1827. Male slaves born after the fourth of July, 1799, were to gain their freedom when they became twenty-eight years old, and female slaves were to be freed after their twenty-fifth birthday.

Belle struggled about the date of her birthday. Although no one was certain of the exact day, the Dumonts agreed that Belle would be eligible for freedom in 1827. One day in 1825, Dumont came to Belle with an offer. First, the master complimented Belle for her hard work during the last fifteen years or more. Two more years remained until he was required by law to set her free. "I'll let you go a year earlier than

BELLE HAULED BUCKETS OF WATER.

the law says, if you promise to work extra hard for me," Dumont said. "And as a bonus, I'll let Tom go free with you. You can live in the cabin that I own down the road." Belle couldn't believe her master's offer. It sounded too good to be true. And it was.

Over the next several months, she put in extra-long hours of hard labor—planting, washing, cooking, cleaning—endless hours of back-breaking work. Then in the spring, Belle accidentally cut her hand on the blade of a scythe. Because Belle didn't slow down and care for the wound, it didn't heal properly. Despite the continual hurt and bleeding from the wound, Belle never missed a day's work. When the year ended, Belle had fulfilled her promise to Dumont. Now she waited for her master to honor his word and give her her freedom.

As 1826 moved on, Dumont still had not freed her; neither had he said a word about the agreement. Belle couldn't stand the waiting any

SHE PUT IN LONG HOURS OF
HARD LABOR.

longer. She burst into the house and confronted the master.

With arrogance in his voice and a wave of his hand, Dumont told Belle, "Our deal is off. Go back to work." When the master had made the offer with Belle, he hadn't known the Hessian fly would kill most of his crops. Now when Belle was confronting Dumont about her freedom, he was facing financial ruin. He needed all of his slaves—especially Belle—to plant the spring crops and make a new start.

Belle was furious at the curt dismissal from her master. "Why won't you honor your word?" she demanded.

At a loss for words, Dumont searched for any excuse. When he noticed her hand still swathed in a bandage, he said, "You can't expect me to free you. With an injured hand, you can't expect me to believe that you've put in extra work."

Belle touched her aching hand, stiff and

"WHY WON'T YOU HONOR YOUR WORD?"

twisted from the year of hard work. Suddenly her anger exploded. She saw a true picture of her master—a little man whose words were mean and meaningless. Without defending her year of hard work, Belle turned and walked away. In her mind, she was a free woman and had stopped being Dumont's Belle. Those days were over!

A year would be too long to wait for her freedom, so Belle decided to run away. She decided, however, that before she left she would finish a job that she had begun: spinning the annual harvest of wool. Because she knew that she couldn't take her children with her when she escaped, she wanted to leave somewhat on good terms with Dumont. Disappointed, Belle realized that the Dumonts' flock of sheep had yielded more wool than normal that year. By the time she finished her spinning, it was late in the autumn of 1826. Nonetheless, she was determined to escape and obtain her freedom!

SHE WOULD FINISH A JOB SHE HAD BEGUN.

"MR. DUMONT HAS CHEATED ME
OUT OF MY FREEDOM."

3

Early one fall morning, Belle gathered together her five children. It was time for a serious talk. With expectation on their faces, the children (Diana, Elizabeth, Hannah, Peter, and baby Sophia, less than a year old) listened quietly to their mother. For years, Belle had worked hard in silence for Dumont and now she had experienced the final blow.

"Mr. Dumont has cheated me out of my freedom, and I'll not let him get away with it," Belle explained to her children. "I've got to run away and I can't take you with me, but I'll be back for you. Someday we'll be together again."

On the morning of her escape, Belle woke up before dawn, gathered together some food and clothing, and put them into a large piece of cloth. Next Belle bundled up Sophia, having decided to take the baby with her. As she slowly walked out of the cabin, Belle knew it would be difficult to leave her other children and Tom, but she knew the other slaves would take good care of them. Belle left the Dumont farm just as the sun was starting to light up the sky. By full daylight, she was far from her master's house.

At the top of a hill, Belle stopped to rest and scanned the horizon. No one was following her, yet she was still troubled. She had no idea where to go or what to do so she could be safe from Dumont. Once again, she prayed for direction. Then Belle remembered Levi Rowe,

SHE WALKED SLOWLY OUT THE DOOR.

who lived down the road from the Dumont estate. Generally Quakers were active abolitionists—a word that Belle had never forgotten.

She decided to ask Rowe for help in her escape. In the early morning light, Belle knocked on his door. It took him a long time to respond because the old man was very ill. In quick bursts of emotion, the frightened runaway slave poured out her story, and Rowe patiently listened.

Rowe was too ill to help her, but he directed her to a Quaker couple named Isaac and Maria Van Wagener. "Maybe they can hide you," the farmer told Belle with concern on his face.

Belle left with fresh hope. Since her childhood, she had known the Van Wageners. A few miles down the road, she reached their home. After hearing Belle's story, the couple welcomed her inside and offered her a job and a place to stay.

"MAYBE THEY CAN HELP YOU."

A short time later, Dumont arrived at the Van Wageners. He had suspected that the Quakers had offered Belle shelter. Confronting his long-time slave, Dumont threatened Belle with harsh punishment for running away at night.

"I did not run away at night," Belle asserted calmly. "I walked away by daylight."

"This argument will not work for you," Dumont disputed. "I insist that you return at once."

When Belle still refused, Dumont tried another tactic. "I know where you are, Belle. When you are not looking, I'll steal Sophia. Then you'll come back."

"No, Mr. Dumont," Belle replied with firmness. "Your threats don't frighten me. I'm not coming back!"

As the Van Wageners watched the struggle between Belle and her master, Mr. Van Wagener offered to buy Belle for $20 and her

"I'M NOT COMING BACK."

baby for $5. The offer was bold because Quakers didn't approve of slavery. Dumont decided to accept Van Wagener's offer, then left in a huff.

"Thank you, Master Van Wagener," Belle said as she addressed her new owner. But the Quaker stopped her and said, "Belle, you and Sophia are free. There is but one Master and He who is your Master is my Master."

Through the winter, Belle stayed and found the Van Wageners were a kind and gentle couple. Sometimes Belle grew homesick, especially when she learned that Mr. Dumont had sold her only son Peter to a Dr. Gedney who planned to take the boy to England as a body servant.

Over the loss of her children, sometimes Belle considered returning to the Dumont estate. Years later, Belle told friends that a powerful force had turned her around whenever she had tried to do so. "Jesus stopped me," she explained simply.

"JESUS STOPPED ME."

One day, Mr. Van Wagener told Belle some distressing news. Dr. Gedney had taken Peter to New York before discovering that the boy was too young to properly serve him. So Dr. Gedney had gone to England alone. Before leaving, however, Dr. Gedney had turned the boy over to his brother, Solomon Gedney, in New Paltz. Solomon, in turn, had sold Peter to a wealthy Alabama planter named Fowler, who had just married their sister Liza.

When Belle heard that Peter was headed to the South, she was furious. Immediately she hurried to the Dumonts and confronted her old master with anger and determination.

"Alabama is a slave-for-life state," Belle said angrily to her former master. "There is no way Peter will ever be free. If you hadn't sold him, he wouldn't be there." Then Belle pleaded with Dumont for his help.

When Mr. Dumont contended that he knew nothing about Peter's movement to Alabama,

BELLE PLEADED WITH DUMONT.

Belle turned to the Quaker abolitionists for help. "Peter's sale was against the law, Belle," they told her at the Van Wageners. "A New York state law forbids selling slaves out of state. If Solomon Gedney would be found guilty, then he would face a fourteen-year jail sentence and/or a stiff financial penalty." Also Peter would immediately be freed.

The Van Wageners recommended that Belle seek help from their friends near Kingston, New York. In the county seat, Belle would need to file a suit against Solomon Gedney. The hostess in Kingston graciously offered Belle supper and a clean bed for the night. As Belle entered the bedroom and shut the door, she was frightened. She had never been offered such a nice, clean, beautiful, and white bed. It never occurred to her to sleep in the bed. For a while she slept underneath the bed, then later she decided that if she didn't use the bed, she might insult her hostess.

SHE SLEPT UNDERNEATH THE BED.

The next morning the family took Belle to the courthouse. Although frightened by the white, clean bed and terrified with the large, imposing stone building, she was determined to get her son back, so she gathered her courage and walked inside. After managing to get directions about where to go and what to do, she filed a complaint against Solomon Gedney who had sold Peter out of the state.

When the grand jury heard Belle's case, they decided in her favor. Belle's Quaker friends helped her hire a lawyer, Esquire Chipp, and he helped Belle make out a writ. Belle resolutely trekked the nine miles from Kingston to New Paltz, where she presented the legal document to the constable of New Paltz. This document ordered Solomon Gedney to appear before the court with Peter.

Unfortunately, the constable served the document on the wrong man, and, with the warning, Solomon Gedney escaped. Gedney's

THE GRAND JURY HEARD BELLE'S CASE.

lawyer counseled him to bring Peter back to New York. To avoid a legal battle, Gedney slipped away to Mobile, Alabama. All Belle could do was wait.

In the spring, Belle heard that Gedney had returned to New Paltz so she went to his home to claim her son. After seeing Belle, Gedney said, "That boy is mine," and slammed the door in her face. Belle refused to back down. She wanted her son free, so she returned to Attorney Chipp. This time, the writ was properly served on the right man. Gedney appeared in court and paid a $600 bond, promising to face the charges that he had sold Peter out of state.

Just when things looked promising, however, Belle met another delay. Attorney Chipp told Belle that her case would have to wait several months until the court was in session again. Belle complained about this new delay, but Chipp asked her to be patient. She said, "I cannot wait. I must have Peter now!" Chipp felt like there was

"I CANNOT WAIT!"

nothing else that he could do on the case so he sent Belle away.

While walking back to the Van Wageners, Belle met a man on the road who asked, "Have they returned your son to you yet?" Belle relayed the latest news to the man.

The man pointed to a nearby stone house, saying, "The lawyer Demain lives there. Go to him and tell him your case with Peter. I think he'll help you with it, but stick with the man and don't give him a moment's peace until he helps you."

After hearing the details of this case, Demain promised to return Peter within twenty-four hours for a fee of $5. Belle's Quaker friends gave her the money, and Demain went to the courthouse. The lawyer quickly returned with some bad news. Peter didn't want to return to his mother. Reportedly, Peter had fallen to his knees and begged to stay with his master.

The next morning, everyone involved in the

DEMAIN PROMISED TO RETURN PETER.

case appeared before the judge in his chambers. "No, she's not my mother!" Peter exclaimed to the judge. "What about that scar on your forehead?" the judge asked. "How did you get that?"

"The Fowlers' horse kicked me," Peter answered.

"And what about this other scar on your cheek? How did that happen?" the judge continued.

"I accidentally ran against a carriage," Peter said, but the judge wasn't fooled with this exhibition from Peter. One look into the boy's eyes made it clear that he was terrified of his master. The answers had been carefully rehearsed.

The judge awarded the boy to his mother. It was official. After Gedney left the room, and when Peter was reassured that he didn't have to accompany his former master, Peter cautiously changed his story. "This woman looks a little like my mother," he admitted.

Belle had won freedom for her son and now took Peter home. That evening as she prepared

"THIS WOMAN LOOKS A LITTLE LIKE MY MOTHER."

Peter for bed, Belle noticed that his back was streaked with old and fresh wounds. "Peter," Belle whispered gently to her son, "what kind of monster would do this to a six-year-old?"

At the question, Peter finally told the truth. It confirmed Belle's suspicions. "Master Gedney told me to say that I didn't know you," Peter explained as tears ran down his cheeks. "He said that if I didn't say what he wanted me to say then I would get the worst whipping I've ever had."

"Now, now child," Belle said as she held her son in her arms, "you're free now and safe with me." As she thought about the events of the last several days, Belle was certain the man on the road who had pointed her to Demain had been an angel from heaven. She thanked God for His answer and Peter's freedom.

Belle didn't think about Peter's freedom in light of the larger picture of U.S. history, that she was one of the first black women in the

"MASTER GEDNEY TOLD ME TO SAY
THAT I DIDN'T KNOW YOU."

United States to win a court case. She was simply a mother happy to be reunited with her son. She prayed, "God, if it be Your will, no child of mine will ever be sold away from me again!"

"NO CHILD OF MINE WILL EVER BE SOLD AWAY FROM ME AGAIN!"

TOM WAS FREED.

4

After Belle had gained Peter's freedom, she stayed in Kingston, New York, where she found work. Peter continued living with Belle, but Sophia, at about age two, went to live with her sisters still on the Dumont estate.

On July 4, 1827, Tom, Belle's husband, was freed along with every other adult slave in the state of New York. Belle stayed in Kingston, and Tom lived in New Paltz. The couple found it impossible to build a home together, and in time they grew apart. Respectfully, they agreed to separate. Until his health failed, Tom did odd jobs in the area, but he died before the end of the year.

Before long, Belle and Peter left Kingston and returned to the Van Wageners. The couple welcomed them back and provided work for Belle. As time passed, Belle became bored with the simple life of the Van Wageners. As the big slave holiday of Pinxter (Pentecost Sunday) approached, Belle thought about giving up her freedom and returning to the Dumont estate where she could sing, drink, smoke, and dance with her slave friends. As her 1850 narrative reports, however, "God revealed Himself to me with all of the suddenness of lightning." She cried out, "Oh, God, how big You be!" Then, being overwhelmed with the greatness of the Divine presence, Belle fell to her hands and knees, trying to crawl away from the Almighty, but she could find no place to hide from His presence.

BELLE FELL TO HER HANDS AND KNEES.

Belle felt the wickedness of her life and the need for someone to speak to God for her. Years later, Belle described this moment as her conversion to Christ. She said later, "I felt Jesus come between God and me as sensibly as I ever felt an umbrella raised over my head." Her voice sounded different and then came a great vision of Jesus Christ. She stated, "I saw the hair on His head, and I saw His cheek; and I saw Him smile, and I have seen the same smile on people since."

Belle admitted that before she had found a relationship with Jesus Christ, she had urged God to kill "all the white people and not leave enough for seed." But after her conversion, she said, "Yeah, God, I love everyone, and the white people, too."

In the evening, when the work for the day was finished, Mr. Van Wagener pulled out his Bible and read aloud to Belle and the others. These lessons from God's Word gave Belle

BELLE SAW A VISION OF JESUS CHRIST.

greater understanding and clarity about the relationship between God and mankind. She recalled those days later in life saying, "Oh, everything at the Van Wageners was so pleasant, and kind and good and all so comfortable; indeed, it was beautiful!"

During these months at the Van Wageners, Peter's body began to heal, but Belle realized that he also needed emotional healing. A happy child, Peter enjoyed running and playing along the wharves in New Paltz. The huge ships that came into the port made great excitement for Peter. He also enjoyed listening to the sailors telling stories of their adventures at sea.

Then Peter began to steal, and when caught, he lied about it. At first, Belle wasn't too hard on her son because of his difficult past, but she knew that she needed to help him. Belle tried to locate a church for Peter, hoping that perhaps with proper religious instruction, Peter wouldn't stray from his mother's teachings.

PETER LISTENED TO THE SAILORS' STORIES.

One Sunday morning, Belle put on her good black dress and dressed Peter for church. Neither one of them had shoes, but Belle decided that shoes didn't matter to God. They arrived at a Methodist meeting held in a private house. Knowing that it was not customary for blacks to enter white meetings unless they sat in a separate "Negro pew," Belle was afraid to enter the house. Instead, she stood outside the house and peered through an open window.

But God gave Belle new strength to enter the church, and the congregation welcomed mother and son to their meetings. While living in Kingston with the Van Wageners, Belle joined a church for the first time. She took her children with her to church as often as possible.

At one of these church meetings, Belle met Miss Geer, a schoolteacher from New York City. Miss Geer was impressed with Peter's inquisitive nature and bright mind. She told Belle, "There are many jobs available in New

BELLE MET MISS GEER, A SCHOOLTEACHER.

York City and a world of opportunities for Peter in terms of his education. You should consider moving when you can."

The thought of leaving the immediate area was a new one for Belle. After Freedom Day, many former slaves had moved to New York City. Nothing was hindering Belle from moving to another city and finding work there, too. It made sense to her that she could possibly find a better paying job and save money for a home. When Belle talked it over with Diana, Hannah, and Elizabeth, they encouraged her to take the opportunity for the sake of Peter and promised to care for their younger sister, Sophia.

At the end of the summer of 1829, Belle and Peter said a tearful goodbye to their family and left New Paltz. They promised to keep in touch with the Van Wageners, then boarded a boat to carry them down the Hudson River. When the boat pulled into the New York City harbor, Belle looked an imposing figure. She

THE BOAT PULLED INTO NEW YORK HARBOR.

stood six feet tall and was dressed in a plain gray dress with a white bandanna tied around her head.

Miss Geer met Belle and Peter at the docks with her carriage. As the carriage bumped over the cobblestone streets, Peter clung to his mother and looked wide-eyed at the new and interesting sights. The busy streets and masses of people were amazing to Belle. She sat straight-backed in her seat and looked the picture of calmness and composure. In reality, however, Belle was extremely frightened. The clutter and the noise of the city bombarded her senses and confused her.

Miss Geer had arranged for Belle to begin working for the Whitings, the Garfields, and later a prominent newspaper family. She enrolled Peter in a navigation school which took advantage of his interest in ships and sailing.

By wandering around the neighborhoods, Belle began to learn her way around New York City. She often listened as people stood talking

PETER CLUNG TO HIS MOTHER.

outside a shop or market. Belle discovered the long-standing free black community in New York City, and she proudly joined their growing ranks. One day, Belle was told that whites and blacks worshiped in separate services at the Methodist Church on John Street. To see it for herself, Belle visited the Mother Zion African Methodist Episcopal (AME) Church. (The AME Church is the oldest African-American organization in the United States.) During her days in New York City, Belle was a beloved member of this AME Church and known for her Spirit-filled prayers and original hymns.

One Sunday after the AME services, a man and a woman approached Belle. The woman told her, "I am your sister Sophia, and this is your brother Michael. We are also the children of Mau Mau Brett and Baumfree. Some of our friends told us that you worship in this church so we came here to find you." Belle was reunited with the brother who had been snatched away on a

"I AM YOUR SISTER."

sled as a child and sold into slavery.

The three siblings spent the entire day talking. Sophia was living in Newburgh, New York, while Michael had moved to New York City. Belle asked about their other sister, Nancy, who had been sold at the same time as Michael.

"Nancy lived here in New York City," Michael said. "In fact, she attended Mother Zion until her recent death." As Michael described Nancy's appearance, Belle shrieked with surprise and delight. Nancy had been one of the elderly mothers and had prayed along side Belle at the altar as well as sung hymns with her. The women had never known that they were sisters.

As Michael, Sophia, and Belle sat in a park together, they cried at how slavery had torn apart their family and their lives. "What is this slavery?" Belle exclaimed. "It can do such terrible things!"

SLAVERY HAD TORN APART HER FAMILY.

Miss Geer invited Belle to join her and some others who went into one of the worst parts of the city, the Five Points area, to tell people about the changing power of Jesus Christ. Belle joined the small group of Christians a few times as they greeted people on the street corners and sang hymns in the street, but Belle wondered why they did it. *These people need food, decent houses, and clothing,* she thought. *There must be a more effective way to show Christ's love.*

When Belle heard about the Magdalene Asylum, a shelter that was for homeless women, she offered her assistance. Elijah Pierson ran the shelter in a large gray house on Bowery Hill. Unknown to Belle and his followers, Pierson was a religious fake. He claimed to run the Magdalene Asylum with instructions directly from God. Such a claim wasn't hard for Belle to believe because she felt God directly guided her decisions and life. Belle liked Pierson and agreed to work part-time and often

THEY SANG HYMNS IN THE STREET.

participated in his religious services.

One Sunday morning, Belle answered the front door of the Asylum. She was startled to see a long-bearded figure in a flowing robe standing before her. "I am Matthias. I am God the Father and have the power to do all things," the man claimed, then asked to see Elijah the Tishbite.

In actuality, Matthias was a middle-aged hustler named Robert Matthews who had arrived in the city with a new scheme to steal money from people. Of course, few suspected his evil plans.

Within months, Pierson and Matthias had become partners in a plan of deceit. Belle listened to these men, and their smooth talk convinced her that they were exactly who they claimed to be—God and Elijah the Prophet. Pierson and Matthias started a community called "The Kingdom" on a farm owned by a married couple named Benjamin and Ann

"I AM MATTHIAS."

Folger. The farm was located near the Hudson River, about thirty miles north of New York City. Although every member donated all their worldly possessions and money into the Kingdom, Pierson and Matthias were the only ones permitted to control the finances. Since Belle didn't have much money, the men accepted her into the group on the basis that she would do the washing, ironing, cooking, and cleaning. For her hard work, Belle gained the privilege of worshiping with the others in the Kingdom. Just as Belle had submitted to authority as a slave, in the Kingdom, Belle submitted to Matthias's authority. Belle accepted him as ordained by God and was devoted to him.

For a while, the members of the community lived in peace and harmony. Then Matthias began to exert complete control over the community. Before long Belle began to tire of the constant bickering and strange religious rituals. She decided that Matthias and Pierson didn't

BELLE WOULD DO THE WASH.

deserve her trust and confidence. Although she had no proof of their dishonesty, Belle prepared to leave.

In August 1834, Belle returned to New York City and, with Miss Geer's help, she got back her old job with the Whiting family. Belle not only learned that Peter had dropped out of school and hired out as a coachman for one of Miss Geer's friends, but she saw that Peter was running around with a rough crowd.

Meanwhile, at the Folgers' farm, Pierson had begun to develop serious seizures. By the summer of 1834, he had become so weak that he often stayed in bed. The community did not call a doctor as that would have been against both Pierson's and Matthias's beliefs. In fact, Matthias believed that diseases were caused by the presence of devils, and that he had the power to cast them out.

Belle returned to get her possessions and tell the Kingdom leaders that she was leaving.

PIERSON OFTEN STAYED IN BED.

After she arrived, Pierson suddenly stiffened and collapsed on the floor. By the next morning, he was dead.

Pierson's relatives and neighbors raised questions about his death. They were already suspicious of the Kingdom, and Matthias had increased their suspicions. The resulting trial turned into a media circus, as every day the newspapers featured stories about the strange religious group and its two leaders who had used money for their own greedy desires.

Subsequently, the Kingdom began to fall apart. Westchester County seized the Folgers' farm, forcing all of the members to move. The Folgers moved back to their house in New York on Third Street. Belle, along with Matthias and his children, moved in with the Folgers.

In September 1834, the Folgers, who were facing business losses and financial trouble, explained to Matthias that they could no longer afford to support the Kingdom. This led to a

THE NEWSPAPERS FEATURED STORIES
ABOUT THE TWO LEADERS.

painful argument between the Folgers and Matthias. Then the Folgers, with the hope that it would encourage Belle to leave, paid her $25 as wages even though this payment went against the Kingdom's policy that everyone served without wages. Still loyal to Matthias, Belle turned over the $25 to him and made it clear that she wanted to stay with him, but Matthias gave the money back to Belle.

The Folgers gave Matthias $530 with the expectation, according to Belle, that he would use it to carry out his dream of buying a farm in the West. In a matter of days, Matthias had left the Folger house and gone home to Albany, preparing to move west. Belle expected to go west with Matthias. On the same day that Matthias left the Folger house, Belle also left, separately, taking her luggage with her. She assumed she left the Folgers on good terms.

Traveling north, Belle visited those of her children who were still at the Dumont estate in

BELLE LEFT WITH HER LUGGAGE.

New Paltz; then she boarded a steamboat on the Hudson River to Albany and Matthias. While in Albany, on about September 21, 1834, Belle was surprised to learn that the Folgers had brought charges against Matthias. The police arrested Matthias for stealing the $530 that Belle had thought the Folgers had given him. Confused and upset, Belle returned to New York City.

Once Matthias had left the Folgers' house, they had complained to the police that Matthias had obtained the money from them under false pretenses. The Folgers had also circulated other charges about the Kingdom. They alleged that Matthias, with Belle's help, had murdered Pierson by serving him poisoned blackberries. Also the Folgers claimed that Matthias and Belle had tried to murder them by serving them poisoned coffee.

With these new charges, the police ordered that Pierson's body be taken out of its grave and

SHE BOARDED A STEAMBOAT.

reexamined by doctors. Although the doctors did not find any clear evidence of poison in the body, they found some unknown but "deadly" substance in it.

For many months, the trial for Matthias dragged on. Finally a judge ruled that Pierson had not been murdered but had died of indigestion from eating too many half-ripe blackberries. Matthias was freed from jail, but having been discredited as a fake, he moved to the West so he could live where he was not known.

Belle, however, gained little victory through the trial. Instead, she felt that three years (from 1832 to 1835) of her life and time had been wasted. In God's economy though, these years were not wasted. Never again was Belle easily taken in by fast-talking men who mistook honesty and sincerity for weakness.

THE TRIAL FOR MATTHIAS DRAGGED ON.

PETER DROPPED OUT OF SCHOOL.

5

Because of Belle's participation in the Kingdom, only her victory in a legal suit against her accusers reestablished her reputation. In a different part of her life, however, a huge battle was brewing. Her son Peter had "gone to seed." When Belle had moved to the Kingdom, leaving Peter in the city, he had dropped out of navigation school and refused to attend grammar school.

The city around Peter burst with violence

but to the young boy the violence looked like a great adventure. Although only eleven years old, Peter was tall for his age so the street thugs accepted him into their group. He liked being with the older boys and foolishly stole things to win their approval.

Several times Peter got into trouble with the police and they threw him into jail. On two different occasions, Belle asked for advances on her salary so she could pay Peter's fines and have him released. She always believed in her son.

Belle found Peter a job in a livery stable. For this job, Peter had to take care of the horses, rake out the stalls, and clean harnesses and bridles. When Peter stole a bridle and sold it on the streets, the boss wasn't willing to show any mercy and pressed charges against him. Belle knew that she had lost control of her son. When the messenger came to tell Belle that Peter had been thrown into the Tombs, New York's

BELLE GOT PETER A JOB IN A STABLE.

dreaded jailhouse, she refused to help. Because Belle had warned Peter over and over, she decided to "give Peter up to God."

The boy couldn't believe his mother's reaction. She had always been there for him. Alone, he was frightened of staying in the jailhouse. After he had spent a day in the jail waiting for his mother who never came, he created a clever plan. Sometimes Peter used the name of Peter Williams. In the city, there was a minister with the same name, so Peter sent a message to his "namesake." For some reason, the elderly Williams decided to help the boy, but first he talked with Belle. Together they agreed that Peter needed discipline and that the best place for that discipline was at sea as a sailor. They convinced the local judge to agree with their plan and sentence Peter to work as a sailor. In August 1839, Peter signed up as a crew member aboard the *Zone of Nantucket*. Soon he sailed away on the ship.

PETER SAILED ON A SHIP.

Belle never saw Peter again. He wrote five letters that she always kept. Years later, she told her biographer, "I have no doubt. I feel sure that Peter has persevered and kept the resolve he made before he left home." But often during the black of the night, Belle would look at the sky and wonder if her scattered children were seeing the same beautiful North Star. (For slaves, the North Star held a special meaning—it pointed to freedom.)

During the 1830s, New York City was a center for the abolitionist movement, especially among the free blacks, and Belle continued to live and work in New York City for Mrs. Whiting. As Belle thought about New York City though, she realized it was a dangerous place for blacks. One of the strongest anti-slavery activities was the management of the Underground Railroad. On the opposing side, however, slave catchers roamed and searched through the streets for blacks who had escaped

SLAVE CATCHERS SEARCHED THE STREET
FOR ESCAPED BLACKS.

slavery in the South. Sometimes free slaves were captured along with the runaway slaves, then smuggled out of the city and into slavery again. Also within the city there was a growing competition for jobs between blacks and European immigrants.

After living fourteen years in or near New York City, Belle decided that New York was no longer the place for her. She felt like it was "a wicked city," a "Sodom." Because of her uneasy feelings, Belle decided that she must leave the city, but she didn't say anything to anyone about her plans. By 1843, all of her daughters had grown up and married—even started their own families—and Belle was about forty-six years old.

Belle decided to become a traveling evangelist. Although it was unusual for women to preach, several other black women in the Northeast were already traveling evangelists.

During one of her times in deep prayer,

BELLE WAS IN DEEP PRAYER.

Belle thought she received a message from God, "Go east." The words troubled her and she wondered if she should follow them, but they came again, "Go east." Belle made a decision to follow the Lord to the east—wherever He took her.

For any woman to just wander and speak as the way opened was unusual and even dangerous, but Belle believed that God had called her to leave behind her unhappy life in New York and to speak for Him. One thing still bothered Belle—her name, Isabella. The name of a slave seemed inappropriate for a person beginning a new life as God's pilgrim. She wanted the name of a free woman.

Calling on God for help, Belle received an answer. She remembered Psalm 39:12 (KJV), "Hear my prayer, O Lord, and give ear unto my cry. . .for I am a stranger with thee, and a sojourner, as all my fathers were." To Belle, Sojourner was an appropriate name for someone

"SOJOURNER."

whom God had called to travel up and down the land, showing the people their sins and being a sign to them. She would call herself "Sojourner."

On June 1, 1843, as the first light shone over the horizon, Belle was already awake and stuffing her few dresses into an old pillowcase. About an hour before she left, she informed the Whitings, for whom she had been working as a live-in domestic, that she was quitting. Her long-term employers, the Whitings, were stunned that Belle was leaving and inquired where she would be staying.

"You're crazy, Belle," Mrs. Whiting responded. "We need you here and this is your home. Why travel to the East?"

But Belle would not stay. She flung her pillowcase of belongings over her shoulder and said, "Farewell, friends, I must be about my Father's business."

First she walked to the ferry which was going

SHE WALKED TO THE FERRY.

to Brooklyn. She paid twenty-five cents for the crossing and continued walking toward Long Island. Nearly seventeen years after her escape from slavery, Belle was once again traveling— except this time, at age forty-six, she was free.

By evening, she had walked outside of the city. Stopping at a Quaker farm, Belle asked for a drink of water. The woman gave it to her and asked for her name.

"My name is Sojourner," Belle stated firmly.

But the name wasn't enough for the woman. "Sojourner what?" she asked, wanting to know a last name.

"My name is Sojourner," Belle repeated, then continued on her trip. But the woman's question continued to nag Belle. *Only slaves don't have a last name,* she thought. *Just like my new first name came from God, I'll ask Him for a last name.* Throughout her life, she had always been Hardenbergh's Belle, Dumont's Belle—always identified by her master's name.

"MY NAME IS SOJOURNER."

In prayer, once again, another Bible verse came into her mind: "And ye shall know the truth, and the truth shall make you free (John 8:32 KJV)."

"I've only got one master now—the God of the universe—and His name is Truth. My name is Sojourner Truth," she said to herself, "because from this day I will walk in the light of His truth." Sojourner Truth was a perfect name for one of God's pilgrims.

"MY NAME IS SOJOURNER TRUTH."

SHE CLIMBED THE PLATFORM
TO SPEAK TO THE PEOPLE.

6

Wearing her black Quaker dress and white shawl, one afternoon Sojourner approached a group and asked if she could speak to them. She climbed the platform and the people gathered to hear this speaker. A black woman speaking publicly was unusual, so curiosity quieted the crowd. Clearly Sojourner was no ordinary woman; she stood tall, strong-boned, and proud.

After this introduction to many different people in the area, Sojourner traveled and spoke from meeting to meeting. People began to whisper, "It must be Sojourner Truth," whenever she appeared at a religious meeting in a new neighborhood.

Once someone asked her to speak about her life as a slave. It marked the first time that Sojourner had spoken to such a large group of white people about her background, but after a prayer and a hymn, she began to speak.

"Children, slavery is an evil thing," Sojourner declared. "They sell children away from their mothers, and then dare the mothers to cry about their loss. What kind of men can do such an evil thing?"

A murmur of agreement sounded through the crowd, and Sojourner could see heads nodding while listening with respect. "My mother and father had eleven other children besides me. Some of my brothers and sisters I've never met because they were sold before I was even born. My poor Mau Mau Brett never stopped

"SLAVERY IS AN EVIL THING."

crying for them." The audience was held captive as Sojourner told the story of her brother and sister being sold from the Hardenbergh estate, then of her meeting the brother much later in New York City.

After several months of traveling, Sojourner arrived in Northampton, a town located along the Connecticut River and in the heart of Massachusetts. Her friends described Sojourner as a "commanding figure" with a dignified manner. She "hushed every trifler into silence," and "whole audiences were melted into tears by her touching stories."

Sojourner visited the Northampton Association of Education and Industry, a cooperative community that operated a silkworm farm and made silk fabric. She was impressed with how the people worked together in such a harmonious way.

The Northampton Association had been founded in 1842, and was lead by two advocates

SHE VISITED A SILKWORM FARM.

of the abolition of slavery, Samuel L. Hill, an ex-Quaker, and George Benson, who was William Lloyd Garrison's brother-in-law. Garrison, who edited an abolitionist weekly in Boston, was a frequent visitor. In the eyes of some people, Garrison was the leader of the anti-slavery movement. This tall, gaunt-faced man made angry speeches, but with gentle eyes. He said, "Prejudice against color is rebellion against God." Garrison's newspaper, *The Liberator,* inspired thousands in the abolitionist movement—especially the community at Northampton.

Although these leaders were nothing like Matthias and Pierson from the Kingdom, Sojourner was cautious before getting involved with them too quickly. Despite her uneasy feelings about a community lifestyle, Sojourner stayed. Her days at Northampton turned into the perfect training ground for her work as an abolitionist and feminist.

THE TALL MAN MADE SPEECHES.

Frederick Douglass was another frequent visitor to the Northampton community. He became an active member of the abolitionist movement and gained a reputation for outstanding speaking. In fact, his voice and perfect diction was so respected that it put him at a disadvantage. Southerners began to spread rumors that Douglass had never been a slave. To prove he wasn't a phony, Frederick wrote his autobiography in 1845 which gave names, dates, and events relevant to his life. Since Sojourner couldn't read *Narrative of Frederick Douglass* herself, someone in Northampton read the book aloud to her.

A few months later Truth attended a nearby camp meeting held in the open fields. As often happened at the camp meetings, young rowdies invaded the meeting to amuse themselves. They hooted to interrupt the services, and boasted that they would burn the tents. The leaders of the meeting threatened the young

THEY HOOTED TO INTERRUPT THE SERVICES.

men, but this only seemed to make them more agitated.

When the rowdies began to shake the tent where Sojourner Truth was located, she caught the fear of the leadership and hid behind a trunk. She reasoned that if the men rushed inside the tent they would single her out and kill her because she was the only black person present. Then as she hid behind the trunk, she wondered whether a servant of the Living God should hide. *Have I not faith enough to go out and quell that mob,* she thought, *when I know it is written, "One shall chase a thousand, and two put ten thousand to flight?"*

Sojourner came out from hiding and invited a few of the camp meeting leaders to go outside with her to calm the mob. When the leaders refused, she went out by herself. She walked to a small rise of ground and, in her loud, powerful voice, started to sing. She sang one of her favorite hymns on the resurrection of Christ,

SOJOURNER CAME OUT FROM HIDING.

beginning, "It was early in the morning."

A few of the rioters gathered around her. During a pause in her singing, she asked them, "Why do you come about me with clubs and sticks? I am not doing harm to anyone."

Some of them answered, "We aren't going to harm you, old woman. We came to hear you sing." Sojourner believed that some of these youths would be open to what she had to say so she began to preach to them. From time to time, they asked questions, and she answered them. Gradually the group calmed.

As the number of young people listening to her grew, they asked her to stand on a nearby wagon so they could see her better. Before stepping up on the wagon, she asked them, "If I step up on it, will you tip it over?" Some of them assured her that if anyone tried such an act, they would knock that person down.

Obliging, Sojourner mounted the wagon, then continued talking and singing. Finally she

SOJOURNER CONTINUED TO SING.

asked them if she sang one more song, would they go away and leave the camp in peace. Some of them agreed. She asked them to say it louder and they said it louder. So she sang another song, then they began to move off, some of their leaders disciplining those who were reluctant to join them, until all of the mob had left the camp grounds. After that single situation, Sojourner decided never to run away again. She developed skill in handling rough crowds.

In 1846, Sojourner made a trip back to New Paltz so she could visit her daughter Diana, who had continued working for the Dumonts after gaining her freedom. John Dumont, her former master, told Belle, "Slavery is the wickedest thing in the world." Sojourner was glad to see the change in the old master.

During her stay in the Northampton community, Sojourner heard lecturers who advocated that women should be given the same political

SOJOURNER HEARD LECTURERS.

and legal rights as men. Recognizing that she and the women's rights speakers were kindred spirits, she decided to join their ranks and take on this new battle for freedom. After all, throughout her entire life, she had struggled with the double burden: being both black and a woman in a society that imposed severe restrictions on both groups.

In the 1840's, a woman in the United States enjoyed few rights. She could not vote or hold political office. For the same job, she was paid far less than a man. When she married, her property and earnings came under her husband's control. As a woman, she could not initiate a divorce, but her husband could divorce her, and she was not permitted even to testify against her husband. If the divorce was granted from the courts, her husband was given the custody of their children. Priests and ministers commonly told women at this time in history that they were inferior to men.

SHE DECIDED TO JOIN THEIR RANKS.

Sojourner identified wholeheartedly with this growing movement for the equality of women. Olive Gilbert, an early feminist and a member of the Northampton society, read Sojourner an article in *The Liberator* which reported on the first Women's Rights Convention in Seneca Falls, New York, from July 19 to 20, 1848. Douglass was the only man to play a prominent role in this convention for women's rights.

As Olive Gilbert read Frederick Douglass's autobiography aloud to Sojourner, she encouraged Sojourner to write her own story. "I'll write it for you," Gilbert volunteered. "You dictate it to me." Garrison also encouraged the publication of Sojourner Truth's story because he saw it would add to the growing number of anti-slavery stories. He offered to print the book and even wrote the introduction to *Narrative of Sojourner Truth: A Northern Slave*.

The book was printed in 1850, the same year that Congress passed a more rigid version

OLIVE GILBERT WAS AN EARLY FEMINIST.

of the Fugitive Slave Act in the Compromise of 1850. Looking back at history, the events which led from this point in history to the Civil War, or the War Between the States, is easy to chart.

In September 1850 Congress passed the famous compromise. This Compromise of 1850 was a key issue which led to great discontentment between the North and the South. California, the second largest state in terms of total area, was admitted to the Union as a free state in exchange for a tougher fugitive slave law to replace the poorly enforced law of 1793. This fugitive slave law required the northern states to return runaway slaves to their masters. This compromise, however, settled nothing. The Southerners continued to hide behind states' rights to slavery and the abolitionists of the North were more determined than ever to fight slavery in the West.

Change was blowing for Sojourner. Because the silkworm business wasn't profitable, the

THE NORTHERN STATES HAD TO
RETURN RUNAWAY SLAVES.

Northampton Association, where she lived, closed its doors. George Benson bought the factory building, and Sam Hill took the silk. Sojourner's increased education about women's rights and the abolitionist movement from her experience at Northampton kept her from being too disappointed with the change. Also, Hill offered to build Sojourner a house so that she'd have some security for her advancing years. Sojourner promised to pay back to Hill the $300 it would cost for the house. She planned to get the money from selling her book.

GEORGE BENSON BOUGHT THE
FACTORY BUILDING.

SOJOURNER SOLD MANY COPIES
OF HER BOOK.

7

William Lloyd Garrison and his associate
Wendell Phillips convinced Sojourner to lend
her splendid speaking voice to the abolitionist
cause. Soon Truth was traveling with other
lecturers throughout New England. While traveling on the lecture circuit, Sojourner sold many
copies of her book and with the proceeds continued to pay on her home in Northampton.

From the time Sojourner joined the lecture circuit, she looked much older than her

fifty-three years. Her black hair had turned gray, her forehead had become deeply lined with wrinkles, and she wore wire-rimmed glasses to help her fading eyesight. For almost every occasion, Sojourner wore a plain black dress and a long white shawl with a white handkerchief wrapped around her head to make a turban. From her appearance, some people guessed that she was in her nineties when, in reality, she was forty years younger.

One evening during a meeting in the late 1850's, Garrison saw his friend Sojourner in the audience and said with a matter-of-fact tone, "Sojourner will say a few words, after which Wendell Phillips will speak."

Truth wasn't prepared to say anything publicly, but she didn't pass up the opportunity. When she stood up, her tall presence commanded attention. As she had done at the camp meetings, she used the strength of her voice to capture the attention of her audience. She began

SHE WORE WIRE-RIMMED GLASSES.

with one of her original hymns. Then, without any fanfare, Truth launched into her speech, making each point simply, yet eloquently. After telling the tragic story of her father's death and her struggle to get her son Peter back, she closed her message by saying, "God will not make His face shine upon a nation that holds with slavery." The crowd applauded and cheered. Some of the people cried while others sat stunned and silent. It was a hard act for even Wendell Phillips to follow, but he was the next speaker.

That evening, Sojourner sold twice as many books as before. She decided to go on a speaking tour to sell books and to spread the "truth" as she understood it. Because many people asked about her hymns, she compiled some of them into a booklet and sold them along with her biography. After each evening of selling books, Sojourner dutifully put aside some of the money to pay for the printing of her book and

THE CROWD APPLAUDED AND CHEERED.

some to pay Sam Hill for building her home.

At a women's rights convention in New York, a group of especially hostile men jeered Truth whenever she spoke. She responded that she knew how much it annoyed them to have a black woman speak about justice and freedom. "Blacks and women," Sojourner said, "have all been thrown down so low that nobody thought we'd ever get up again. . .but we will come up again, and now here I am."

This kind of unyielding attitude toward compromise eventually enabled Truth and other feminists to bring about some reforms for women. Sojourner proclaimed the truth in simple terms: For people who had sound logic, racism and sexism were unacceptable.

From her travels and speeches, Sojourner Truth's fame and stature grew as an abolitionist and feminist who had wit and wisdom. Time and time again, she demonstrated her courage as she traveled through New Jersey, New York, Ohio,

"NOBODY THOUGHT WE'D EVER
GET UP AGAIN."

Indiana, Michigan, and the other states she visited. Her powerful voice blended tones of pride and modesty. Her expressed affection for all sympathizers, addressing her audience as "children" and individuals as "honey," endeared her to many people. Her salty wit, which was already characteristic of her speaking style, delighted hearers on many occasions. Sometimes she coined new expressions, for example, instead of saying that every person had to stand on his own two feet, Sojourner said, "Every tub has to stand on its own bottom."

Truth had the ability to appeal to white people by shaming them or encouraging them or even complimenting them. She was one of the few black people who spoke almost exclusively to white people, whether individually or in groups, and few blacks worked as closely as she did with the white abolitionists. A number of incidents demonstrated her talent for subduing racist mobs and destroying racist arguments. She could deal

SHE SUBDUED RACIST MOBS.

with white people from all persuasions.

When Sojourner was about sixty years old, she deemed it time to retire and enjoy the life she'd dreamed of for years. Thus, in 1857, Truth sold her Northampton house for $750 and moved to Harmonia, Michigan, a short distance from Battle Creek.

In 1857, fifty-four other African Americans lived in the Battle Creek area, and the mayor was a conductor on the Underground Railroad. The people in the town felt pleased and honored to have such a famous person living among them. They helped Sojourner change an old barn on College Street into a comfortable house. There Truth planned to spend her final days enjoying her grandchildren.

From her initial days in Harmonia, Sammy Banks, Elizabeth's son from her second marriage, favored his grandmother. He begged to stay with her, and Sojourner welcomed his companionship. When he was young, Sammy

THE MAYOR WAS A CONDUCTOR ON
THE UNDERGROUND RAILROAD.

ran errands and did various chores for his grandmother. Then when Sammy learned to read, he
read the Bible to Sojourner. In many ways,
Sammy became a substitute for Sojourner's lost
son, Peter.

For many days, Sojourner was content to sit
on the front porch, telling stories, singing
hymns, and smoking her white clay pipe. Once
Truth had been criticized for smoking a pipe, a
habit that she had picked up as a child working
for the Schryvers in New Paltz. "The Bible tells
us that no unclean thing can enter the Kingdom
of Heaven," this person told Sojourner.

"True," she responded, "but when I go to
Heaven, I expect to leave my breath behind me."

Against her daughter's protest, Sojourner
prepared for another speaking tour. Before she
left, she had her autobiography updated and
designed a postcard with her photograph on it.
She planned to sell this postcard, along with her
book and hymns, at her meetings. At the bottom

SHE DESIGNED A POSTCARD WITH
HER PHOTOGRAPH ON IT.

of the card were the words, "I sell the shadow to support the substance." Then, taking Sammy with her, Sojourner began this speaking tour at the age of sixty-two.

After traveling for a year, Frances Titus volunteered to become Sojourner's traveling companion and "manager." Together the two women spoke to anti-slavery groups. Truth told audiences, "Slavery must be destroyed, root and branch."

"SLAVERY MUST BE DESTROYED."

HER GRANDSON READ HER ARTICLES
ABOUT LINCOLN.

8

Although Sojourner was illiterate, her grandson, Sammy, kept her well informed about the political affairs of the day, such as the upcoming presidential election. Sojourner was particularly interested in Abraham Lincoln and the new Republican Party. She asked her grandson to read articles about Lincoln whenever he found them. Sojourner liked what she learned about the former Illinois congressman, as well as his stance on the slavery issue. When Lincoln had been a congressman, he had introduced a bill providing for the gradual emancipation of slaves in Washington, D.C. He opposed the opening of territories to slavery. Sojourner was convinced that Lincoln would be a good president.

Lincoln's victory in the November election sparked a wide-scale rebellion in the South. By February 1861, seven states had broken off from the Union and formed their own Confederate government. Four of the other eight slave states soon joined the Confederacy, and the North and the South prepared for war. On April 12, 1861, the Civil War broke out when the Confederate units attacked the Union troops stationed at Fort Sumter, in Charleston, South Carolina.

Sojourner was in Michigan when she got the word that a rebel general had fired on Fort Sumter. She hadn't wanted a war, but once it started, she gave her full support to the Union soldiers.

The Union created the 54th Massachusetts

CONFEDERATE UNITS ATTACKED
THE UNION TROOPS.

Volunteer Infantry as a "test" for the black soldiers' ability in combat. The men of the 54th proved that they could be excellent combat soldiers. The African-American response to the 54th was phenomenal. From all over the country, young blacks came to Boston and signed up. Two of Douglass's sons joined along with James Caldwell, age nineteen, one of Sojourner's grandsons.

One October day in 1862, Josephine Griffing, a feminist and abolitionist friend of Sojourner's, came to visit her in Michigan. For the better part of a year, Josephine and Sojourner had traveled throughout Ohio sharing hardships and triumphs.

"I've come to beg your help," Griffing said. "As you know, the president promised to free the slaves the first part of the year. The war effort is not going well. . .anti-slavery speakers are needed more than ever to rally people to our cause. I have been asked to go into Indiana, and I want you to come with me."

Sojourner smiled and answered, "Let me

THEY WERE EXCELLENT COMBAT SOLDIERS.

get my hat." Throughout the rest of 1862, Josephine and Sojourner traveled together and urged people to push for the end of slavery.

Often Josephine and Sojourner's meetings in Indiana were disrupted with loud and insulting shouts of, "Down with you!" "We think the niggers have done enough!" "We will not hear you speak!" "Stop your mouth!" Sojourner's friends were concerned for her safety, but she assured them that she felt safe because truth is powerful and will prevail.

On January 1, 1863, President Abraham Lincoln signed an executive order, called the Emancipation Proclamation, that ended slavery in the rebel states. The Proclamation said, "All persons held as slaves within any State or designated part of a State the people whereof shall then be in rebellion against the United States shall be then, thenceforward, and forever free."

The Proclamation was received across the North with cheers and tears. Thousands of

PRESIDENT LINCOLN SIGNED
AN EXECUTIVE ORDER.

churches rang their church bells. People danced in the streets. Sojourner gathered her friends in Battle Creek and celebrated with cheering, singing, and long speeches.

Because Truth had been active all her life, sitting still was almost impossible for her. Besides, now was no time for a seasoned abolitionist to quit. Sojourner plunged into her work again, even though her daughters urged her at least to slow down. "There's a war going on," Sojourner defended herself, "and I mean to be a part of it."

In the beginning of the Civil War, blacks had not been accepted as soldiers in the Union army. After the Emancipation Proclamation was issued, however, the North began to recruit blacks to serve in racially segregated units. Fifteen hundred black troops enlisted in the 1st Michigan Volunteer Black Infantry. Although these black soldiers weren't paid the same as whites and sometimes were mistreated by their

CHURCH BELLS RANG.

white officers, they continued fighting courageously for the cause of freedom. Sojourner spoke out against the injustice these soldiers endured, pointing out that if black soldiers were dying equally, they should be paid equally for living.

By Thanksgiving 1863, Sojourner was told that her grandson, James Caldwell, was missing in action. He had not been seen since the morning of July 16, 1863, when the 54th had seen action on Majes Island. Two days later the regiment had attacked Fort Wagner, South Carolina. From the *Standard*, Sammy read the details to Sojourner, "The Charleston papers all say that six hundred and fifty of our dead were buried on the Sunday morning after the assault. . . . Unofficial reports say the Negroes have been sold into slavery and that white officers are treated with immeasurable abuse."

What about James? Truth wondered about her grandson. Was he lying in a common grave

THE 54TH REGIMENT ATTACKED
FORT WAGNER.

with others or was he suffering a fate worse than death—slavery?

During the spring of 1864, Sojourner, though only recently recovered from a long illness, decided to visit President Lincoln in Washington, D.C. Many of her abolitionist friends believed President Lincoln was moving too slowly to bring about an end to slavery, but Truth greatly respected the President. "Have patience!" she told them. "It takes a great while to turn about this great ship of state." In the meantime, she believed that Lincoln could use some encouragement.

Until the day of her departure, Sojourner didn't tell anyone about her plans. She was working as a laundress for a Battle Creek family. "I've got to hurry with this washing," Truth told her employers. When they asked why she was so pressed for time, she replied, "Because I'm leaving for Washington this afternoon. I'm going down there to advise the president."

"I'VE GOT TO HURRY WITH THIS WASHING."

Accompanied by her grandson, Sammy Banks, Sojourner boarded the train for the nation's capital, stopping in several towns along the route to give speeches. In September 1864, she reached Washington, D.C. In a little more than a month, Americans would vote about whether President Lincoln would serve a second term of office.

Parts of Washington reminded Truth of the Five Points district in New York City. The streets of Washington were filled with slaves who had poured into the city after their freedom. They lived in unhealthy conditions, surrounded by despair and filth. Sojourner's heart went out to these blacks, and she helped them whenever she could.

Freeing the slaves had created a dilemma: What was to be done with the millions of people without education or money but who had limited skills? Knowing Congress had set aside funds to establish the Freedman's Bureau,

SOJOURNER BOARDED THE TRAIN.

which was designed to help the freed slaves make the transition from slavery to freedom, Sojourner hoped that there might be a job for her within the Bureau.

When Sojourner learned that her good friend and former traveling companion, Josephine Griffing, was in Washington, she went to see her right away. Griffing had become the local agent of the National Freedman's Relief Association. Truth expressed her concern about the condition of the newly freed slaves. Josephine said, "I know just the place for you. Freedman's Village."

Constructed by the army as a model village, Freedman's Village was in Arlington, Virginia, just outside Washington. The series of neat cottages was a great improvement over the shacks the slaves had lived in during slavery. Later Sojourner learned that the village was located on the old estate of General Robert E. Lee.

Truth, along with her grandson, Sammy, moved into the village. Sojourner moved

TRUTH AND SAMMY MOVED INTO THE VILLAGE.

around the village like a woman half her age. She helped the other women learn how to sew, cook, clean, comb hair, and take care of their children. Sojourner sent Sammy to the village school and encouraged mothers to send their children as well as to attend adult classes for themselves.

One day Truth found a group of frightened women huddled together, crying. White men had stolen their children and made them work without pay. "Fight the robbers," Sojourner told them forcefully. "You're free now. Don't let anyone treat you like slaves!"

One of the white men, who was from Maryland, tried to intimidate Truth with threats. "Old woman," he growled, "stay out of our affairs or we'll put you in jail."

The words didn't budge the seasoned warrior. She told him, "If you try anything like that, I shall make the United States rock like a cradle." The men left Sojourner alone and stopped

"YOU'RE FREE NOW."

raiding Freedman's Village to steal children.

Even though Sojourner had been in Washington, D.C. for several months already, she still hadn't managed to schedule a meeting with President Lincoln. When she'd arrived, she had tried to secure an appointment with Lincoln but found that on her own, she had been unable to do so. Then Truth asked Lucy Colman—a white, Massachusetts-born abolitionist whose permanent home was in Rochester, and who at the time was teaching freed slaves in Washington—to arrange an appointment for her. Colman admired Truth and was willing to help her. After some time, Colman succeeded in obtaining an appointment. When Colman finally took Truth to the White House on October 29, 1864, the two women had to wait several hours for their turn to see the busy president.

From time to time as the women waited, the president appeared to usher someone into his office. Truth was pleased to see that he extended

LUCY COLMAN WAS TEACHING
FREED SLAVES IN WASHINGTON.

the same courtesy to his black guests as he did to his white visitors.

Finally, Truth and Colman entered the President's office. Truth had planned to speak with him about improving the conditions of former slaves, but when she was introduced to the President, she noted his weary face. His shoulders seemed to sag heavily under the burden they carried. Sojourner's heart was moved with the great sadness of this man who had freed her people. She decided not to add another complaint to his load. Instead, she kept the conversation light.

After she sat down, Sojourner told him bluntly, "I never heard of you before you were put in for president."

Lincoln laughed, then replied, "I heard of you years and years before I ever thought of being president. Your name is well known in the Midwest."

President Lincoln showed her around his office and pointed out a Bible that a group of

"YOUR NAME IS WELL KNOWN IN THE MIDWEST.

Baltimore blacks had presented to him. She held the Book in her hands and traced the big gold letters—*The Bible*—with her finger. Although Sojourner couldn't read the Book, she treasured every word in it.

Sojourner thanked the President for all his efforts to help black Americans and advised him not to worry about the blustering attacks of his critics because she thought the people in the nation were behind him and would support him in the upcoming election. Lincoln, in turn, thanked Truth for her encouragement. When it was time to leave, Sojourner asked Lincoln to sign her "Book of Life." For Sojourner, the "Book of Life" was a combination scrapbook and autograph book. Throughout her travels, she collected the signatures of great people she met and respected. She also kept personal letters and newspaper clippings. Everywhere Sojourner went, she took her "Book of Life" with her.

She watched with great pride as the President

SHE HELD THE BOOK IN HER HANDS.

signed, "For Aunty Sojourner Truth, A. Lincoln, October 29, 1864." (Years later, the terms, "Aunty" and "Uncle," became words that black women and men resented. During the time of Lincoln, however, they were terms of endearment. For instance, General William T. Sherman was affectionately known as "Uncle Billy," and General Robert E. Lee's soldiers called him "Uncle Bobby.")

In November, as Sojourner had predicted, Lincoln was swept back into office with an overwhelming margin in the wake of several victories from the Union army. By this time, Sojourner had discovered that she enjoyed the busy atmosphere in the nation's capital, and thus was still working at the Freedman's Village when General Robert E. Lee surrendered to General Ulysses S. Grant at Appomattox Court House in Virginia on April 9, 1865. The surrender officially ended the war—more than half a million people had paid with their lives.

GENERAL ROBERT E. LEE
WAS CALLED "UNCLE BOBBY."

Six days after the surrender, President Lincoln's name was added to the list of victims. A freezing drizzle was falling in Washington the night it was announced that Lincoln had been assassinated during a play at the Ford Theater. An actor, John Wilkes Booth, had shot the President. After the shooting, Lincoln was taken to the home of William Peterson at 453 Tenth Street, where he died at 7:22 A.M.

That same evening in a separate incident, Secretary of State William Steward was stabbed, but he survived. Vice President Andrew Johnson became the President of the United States. Truth, who believed that no one had done more for the cause of black Americans than Lincoln, was among those who were devastated by his sudden death.

Thousands of people, including Sojourner and Sammy, walked through the East Room of the White House where Lincoln's body lay in state. For the last time, Sojourner looked at the

**THOUSANDS OF PEOPLE WALKED
THROUGH THE EAST ROOM.**

President who would be remembered as "the Emancipator."

In the month that followed Lincoln's death, the last of the Confederate armies surrendered to Union forces. The Civil War was finally over. The battle against slavery had spanned four years and taken hundreds of thousands of lives, but it had been won. By the end of the war nearly ten percent of Union troops were black soldiers. Truth's prayers had been answered. She had lived to see the end of slavery. On December 12, 1865, Truth and millions of other Americans celebrated as Congress ratified the Thirteenth Amendment to the Constitution. This amendment declared that "neither slavery nor involuntary servitude . . .shall exist within the United States or place subject to their jurisdiction." A little more than two and a half centuries after it had been established in America, slavery had at last officially ended.

Sammy and Sojourner continued to live at

THE CONFEDERATE ARMIES SURRENDERED.

the Village. By this time, Sojourner's grandson, James Caldwell, who had been missing in action because he had been taken prisoner during a battle, had returned home from the Civil War.

One day as Sojourner and her white friend, Mrs. Laura Haviland, were boarding a streetcar together, Sojourner boarded ahead of her friend. The conductor rudely snatched her out of the way. "Let the lady on before you," he snapped.

"I'm a lady, too," Sojourner snapped back. The conductor pushed Truth off the streetcar saying, "Get off!"

Mrs. Haviland stopped the man. "Don't you put her off," she demanded.

"Why? Does she belong to you?" the conductor said angrily.

"No," Mrs. Haviland replied unflinchingly. "She belongs to humanity."

"Then take her and go!" Then the conductor slammed Sojourner against the door and

"GET OFF!"

bruised her shoulder. After Truth asked Mrs. Haviland to note the number of the car, the conductor left them alone. "It is hard for the old slave-holding spirit to die," Truth reflected, "but die it must."

At the hospital, when Truth and Haviland asked a surgeon to examine Truth's shoulder, he found it swollen. The two women reported the incident to the president of the streetcar company. He promptly fired the conductor from his job.

This company president advised Truth to have the conductor arrested for assault, which she did with the help of the Freedman's Bureau who furnished her with a lawyer. A few days later, Justice William Thompson held a hearing for the conductor, as reported in a curious article published in at least four Washington newspapers.

Sojourner won her case in court. As she described the impact of the incident, "Before the trial was over, so many blacks were daring

THE SURGEON EXAMINED TRUTH'S SHOULDER.

to ride in the cars that the inside of the cars looked like pepper and salt." Soon the conductors who had cursed Sojourner for wanting to ride would stop for black and white ladies and even condescend to say, "Walk in, ladies." More directly, Sojourner later claimed that her Washington ride-ins had changed Washington. Conductors stopped to pick up passengers regardless of their color. The old warrior had marked another victory in her struggle for equality.

"THE INSIDE OF THE CARS LOOKED LIKE
PEPPER AND SALT."

SHE SANG SEVERAL OF HER ORIGINAL SONGS.

9

Sojourner's victory over the streetcar was short-lived. Soon laws were passed across the nation which made it illegal for blacks and whites to ride together. These laws, known as "Jim Crow" laws, stayed in effect until the modern civil rights movement.

Speaking in Detroit in the campaign for the reelection of President Grant in 1872, Sojourner was about seventy-five years old. She "sang several of her original songs, all of which," according to the newspaper, "were received with applause." When she was speaking in a small Pennsylvania town in 1874, a newspaper reported that Sojourner sang "right sweetly a Negro melody. . .giving just enough of a Southern Negro double-demi-semi-quaver to it to make it interesting."

A newspaper from Springfield declared, "We do most decidedly dislike the complexion and everything else appertaining to Mrs. Truth, the radical—the renowned, saintly, liberated, oratorical, pious slave. . . . She is a crazy, ignorant, repelling Negress, and her guardians would do a Christian act to restrict her entirely to private life."

Despite these attacks which showed the poorest side of society during this period, Sojourner refused to give up her fight to get land for the indigent black people. Her advancing age, precarious health, and the threats and jibes of people notwithstanding, Truth continued

SOJOURNER REFUSED TO GIVE UP HER FIGHT.

to travel and preach. She passed through Massachusetts, western New York, Michigan, Kansas, Iowa, Illinois, Missouri, Wisconsin, Washington, Ohio, New Jersey, and Kentucky during the last ten years of her life. On each of these trips, she met with old and new friends, sang her songs, and continued entertaining and enlightening people on a variety of topics—all of them connected to the well-being and liberation of black people and women. Black progress continued to be blocked, however, by conservative whites. More and more, Truth began to realize that the battle for black freedom had only begun.

At last, Sojourner decided to return home—home to Michigan. She missed Battle Creek and her family there, but more importantly Sammy was ill. At first the illness didn't seem serious, but his fever grew worse along with his cough. Due to her favorite grandson's illness, Sojourner grew depressed, and then developed an ulcer on her leg. When Sammy died in February 1875,

SAMMY DIED IN FEBRUARY 1875.

her condition worsened. Sammy hadn't even reached his twenty-fifth birthday. To Sojourner, Sammy's death was worse than losing her son Peter because Sammy had been such a good and faithful companion. She never stopped mourning his death.

No matter what Sojourner did, she couldn't work away her hurt. She missed Sammy terribly and without him felt handicapped, because he had read to her, taken care of all her correspondence, and looked after her affairs. Truth had written her family that she was going back to Battle Creek to die, but she outlived her grandson by nine years.

Rumors began to circulate that Sojourner had died or that she was too old to travel, having already celebrated her hundredth birthday. Actually she was nearing eighty years old and living at her home in Battle Creek. Although her hair had already turned gray thirty years before, now her hearing and sight had almost disappeared. To

SOJOURNER LIVED AT HER HOME
IN BATTLE CREEK.

walk, Sojourner needed the support of a cane.

In 1877, according to some accounts, Truth's health mysteriously improved. The next year, Sojourner went on another speaking tour which covered thirty-six different towns in Michigan. Then, at the age of eighty-one, she was one of three Michigan delegates to the Woman's Rights Convention in Rochester. Later, after a grueling trip to Kansas, where she spoke to newly freed slaves who were planning to homestead, Sojourner returned home for good.

By the beginning of 1882, Truth had become gravely ill. Painful ulcers began to cover her arms and legs, and she became too weak to get up from bed. She remained this way for the next year and a half. According to Olive Gilbert, "Her life's forces were spent."

Dr. John Harvey Kellogg, director of the Battle Creek Sanitarium, admitted her because she was near death. Even in her pain and close to

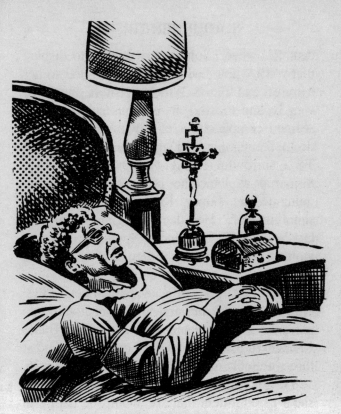

SHE BECAME TOO WEAK TO GET UP FROM BED.

death, however, Sojourner was able to display that spirit which had become so familiar to her admirers and friends. With her visitors, she spoke weakly and mostly on religious subjects. She seemed completely at ease with her imminent death, feeling that God's glory was awaiting her. To a sorrowful friend who paid her a visit, Sojourner explained her peace, saying, "I'm not going to die, honey. I'm going home like a shooting star." Her deeply ingrained faith in God's goodness convinced Sojourner that she would return to the sky and go directly to God's bosom.

One morning early in November, 1883, Gilbert visited Truth and found her in extreme pain. Two weeks later, at her home in Battle Creek, Truth sank into a deep coma. She died at three o'clock in the morning, November 26, 1883. She did not fear death, she had said, for she was confident that she would be happy in heaven.

TRUTH SANK INTO A DEEP COMA.

Many people around her were misled as to her age. Some believed that she was almost a second Methuselah: one of them said that she was eighty-two as early as 1868; when she met with President Grant and the senators in 1870, she was reportedly ninety; close to death she herself declared that her age was 114; her obituary put it as 108; on her gravestone, which was carved years later, appeared the age, 105. In fact, when Sojourner Truth died in 1883, she was about eighty-six years old.

Two days after her death, nearly a thousand people gathered at her house and formed a procession behind the black-plumed hearse that bore her body. The sun was setting in Battle Creek's Oakhill Cemetery as Truth was lowered into her final resting place. A crimson and gold sky lit up the western horizon.

Nearly eighty years after her death, a historical marker was finally placed at her grave from the Sojourner Truth Memorial Association of

NEARLY A THOUSAND PEOPLE
GATHERED AT HER HOUSE.

Battle Creek. This memorial association had been formed in the 1920's for the purpose of raising five thousand dollars to perpetuate Sojourner's name. Dissolved during the 1930's, the group reappeared later under different leadership and was responsible for providing the funds for both the historical marker and the Sojourner Truth Room in Battle Creek's Kimball House Museum.

Once Truth said, "I never determined to do anything and failed." That belief was the most essential statement about her life. From the moment she walked off John Dumont's farm, Sojourner Truth had absolute confidence in the rightness of her acts and in her ultimate triumph over the most imposing of obstacles.

If Sojourner had not believed passionately in the justice of the struggle for black freedom, she would not have devoted her life to the cause of truth. The spirit of Sojourner Truth and her cause of freedom continues to live today.

SOJOURNER
TRUTH
MEMORIAL

A MEMORIAL ASSOCIATION WAS
FORMED IN THE 1920s.

SOJOURNER TRUTH

Whenever people speak out against injustice and scorn oppression, the dreams and ideals of Sojourner Truth continue to live. Whenever people defend the downtrodden or weak, the dreams and ideals of Sojourner Truth endure. Whenever people act on their belief in equality, freedom, and justice, they keep the ideals of Sojourner Truth alive in the hearts of mankind.

THE DREAMS AND IDEALS OF
SOJOURNER TRUTH WILL ENDURE.

AWESOME BOOKS FOR KIDS!

The Young Reader's Christian Library
Action, Adventure, and Fun Reading!

This series for young readers ages 8 to 12 is action-packed, fast-paced, and Christ-centered! With exciting illustrations on every other page following the text, kids won't be able to put these books down. Over 100 illustrations per book. All books are paperbound. The unique size (4 ⅛" x 5 ⅜") makes these books easy to take anywhere!

A Great Selection to Satisfy All Kids!

Abraham Lincoln	*Heidi*	*The Pilgrim's Progress*
Ben-Hur	*Hudson Taylor*	*Pocahontas*
Billy Graham	*In His Steps*	*Pollyanna*
Billy Sunday	*Jesus*	*Robinson Crusoe*
Christopher Columbus	*Jim Elliot*	*Roger Williams*
Corrie ten Boom	*Joseph*	*Ruth*
Daniel	*Little Women*	*Samuel Morris*
David Brainerd	*Luis Palau*	*The Swiss Family*
David Livingstone	*Lydia*	*Robinson*
Deborah	*Miriam*	*Thunder in the Valley*
Elijah	*Moses*	*Wagons West*
Esther	*Paul*	
Florence Nightingale	*Peter*	

Available wherever books are sold.

Or order from: Barbour Publishing, Inc., P.O. Box 719
Uhrichsville, Ohio 44683
http://www.barbourbooks.com

$2.50 each retail, plus $1.00 for postage and handling per order. Prices subject to change without notice.